Presented To

Bobbie

Date

Easter 2014

from mommy and Scot!
we love you so much!

for
Mothers and Daughters

Little Girls Bible Storybook

for Mothers and Daughters

Carolyn Larsen
Illustrated by Caron Turk

BakerBooks

a division of Baker Publishing Group
Grand Rapids, Michigan

Text © 1998, 2014 by Carolyn Larsen
Illustrations © 1998 by Caron Turk

Published by Baker Books
A division of Baker Publishing Group
P.O.Box 6287, Grand Rapids, MI 49516-6287
www.bakerbooks.com

Printed in China

Library of Congress Cataloging-in-Publication Data
Larson, Carolyn, 1950–
    Little girls Bible storybook for mothers and daughters / Carolyn Larsen ; illustrated by Caron Turk.
      pages cm
    Summary: Forty-six stories, imaginatively told from the perspective of the woman who lived each experience.
    ISBN 978-0-8010-1547-2 (cloth)
    1. Bible stories, English. I. Turk, Caron, illustrator. II. Title.
BS551.3.L3735 2014
220.95′05—dc23   2013007779

Scripture quotations are from GOD'S WORD®. © 1995 God's Word to the Nations. Used by permission of Baker Publishing Group.

14   15   16   17   18   19   20   7   6   5   4   3   2   1

Contents

Dear Moms,

Have you ever thought about the feelings or emotions of the characters who actually lived our favorite Bible stories? The Bible doesn't often tell us what these people were thinking or feeling, so when we read these stories we may forget that they are about real people—who had struggles and questions, fears and hopes, just as we do today.

The Little Girls Bible Storybook provides an opportunity to look at well-loved Bible stories through the eyes and hearts of the women who lived them. Of course, we don't really know what these long-ago women were actually feeling, but by thinking about what they may have felt, we can have a deeper insight into the lessons they learned. We can learn from their experiences by imagining what a woman of today may have felt in those same situations.

Caron Turk has wonderfully illustrated these stories, and I know that you will enjoy her whimsical style. You and your daughter can have fun looking for the darling little angel with the pink-dotted wings who is hiding in each illustration.

My hope is that these stories will make familiar Bible characters more real to you and your daughter, and that the questions and thoughts in the Becoming a Woman of God section will provide some great conversation starters. Hopefully, you will find opportunities to tell your daughter things about your life that she may not know.

God bless you and your little girl as you read The Little Girls Bible Storybook for Mothers and Daughters.

Carolyn Larsen

Eve's Awakening

Genesis 1–2

"Eve, wake up," the gentle voice whispered.

"Who's there?" Eve mumbled, stretching her arms and wiggling her toes for the very first time.

"It's God, your Creator. Open your eyes, sweet child.

Eve opened her eyes. She couldn't believe what she saw. "It's so beautiful!" Eve ran through the garden, touching things for the very first time. "What are these?" she cried, pointing at a mound of color.

"Flowers," God answered. "Smell them."

"Mmmmm, they smell sweet!" Eve giggled. She heard something behind her. "What's that noise?"

"A waterfall," God said, enjoying her discoveries.

Eve leaned over the water and laughed out loud. "It tickles when it splashes me."

"Look, there's someone in the water!"

"No, sweet child, that's your reflection. You're looking at you," God explained. "Come over here; I want you to meet Adam." Eve looked shyly at the tall man across from her.

"He looks nice," she whispered to their Creator.

"He is," God said, smiling. "Adam, this is Eve. She will be your wife."

And the Lord God planted a garden toward the east in Eden

"She looks nice," Adam whispered.

"She will be a good helper for you," God said. "I made you both to be a lot like me. You can talk, and think, and make decisions, just like I do. You will be very happy together."

Becoming a Woman of God

God created girls in his image.

Eve was made in God's image. That means God made her to be like him.

You are made in God's image too! He made you to be exactly the girl he wants you to be.

Mom, help your little girl think of special things about herself. Talk about how kind or helpful she is. Help her see how she is made in God's image.

A Verse to Remember

You alone created my inner being.
You knitted me together inside my mother.

Psalm 139:13

The First Sin

Genesis 3

"Pssst, hey, over here, lady!"

Eve stopped eating and looked around. Seeing no one, she took another big bite. Suddenly a snake dropped down right in front of her. "Oh, you scared me," Eve said. "Who are you?"

"Never mind," the snake hissed. "Why are you eating that? You could have the sweetest fruit in the garden."

"Which fruit are you talking about?" Eve asked.

"It's on that tree in the center of the garden," the snake hissed.

"But God said not to eat that fruit," said Eve.

"Trust me, it's the sweetest, juiciest fruit in the whole garden."

"You make it sound so good," Eve said.

"God didn't really mean that you shouldn't eat that fruit. Come on, try it!"

Eve looked at the fruit, then at the snake. Suddenly she grabbed the fruit and took a bite.

This was a sad day for Adam and Eve

"Adam, try this," Eve called. "It tastes so good."

"That fruit is from the tree God told us to stay away from," Adam replied. But he couldn't resist taking a bite of it too.

Adam and Eve couldn't hide their sin from God. It was hard to face his disappointment. "I'm sorry you disobeyed me. It means you have to leave this beautiful garden," God said.

The Lord God sent Adam and Eve from the garden.

Eve cried as they left the garden. "I'm sorry. I didn't mean to disobey—the snake made the fruit sound so good."

"I know, child, I know," God said. "I have to punish you for disobeying, but I still love you. I always will."

Becoming a Woman of God

Bad choices have consequences.

Eve made a bad choice when she disobeyed God. Disobedience means punishment. That is the consequence. Eve was punished for her bad choice.

Mom, talk with your little girl about a time she made a bad choice. Was she punished for it? How did she feel about that?

A Verse to Remember

Now that we have God's approval by faith, we have peace with God because of what our Lord Jesus Christ has done.

Romans 5:1

Noah's Ark

Genesis 6:1–7:9

"You're going to build a what?" Mrs. Noah asked.

"An ark," Mr. Noah repeated. "A boat, my dear! A big, big boat!"

"A boat? Where did you get that idea?" she asked.

"From God," Noah replied.

Mrs. Noah brushed the flour from her hands as Noah explained that God was tired of the way people were behaving.

"God has decided to wipe out every living thing," Noah explained. "Then God will begin the human race again—with us."

"Well," said Mrs. Noah, "God has given you a big job. You had better get busy."

Noah's three married sons and their wives were going on the ark with Noah and his wife. As Noah put the finishing touches on the ark, there was a loud clomping sound. Mrs. Noah looked up and saw a parade of animals coming toward them. "Noah! What's going on here?" she cried.

"God is sending animals—two of every kind—to go in the ark with us," Noah replied.

"With us? We're going in the boat with those wild animals?" Mrs. Noah asked.

"We'd better. The flood is coming."

Mrs. Noah looked at the lions, bears, and spiders (did there have to be spiders?). She smiled and took Noah's hand. "Well, let's get going then."

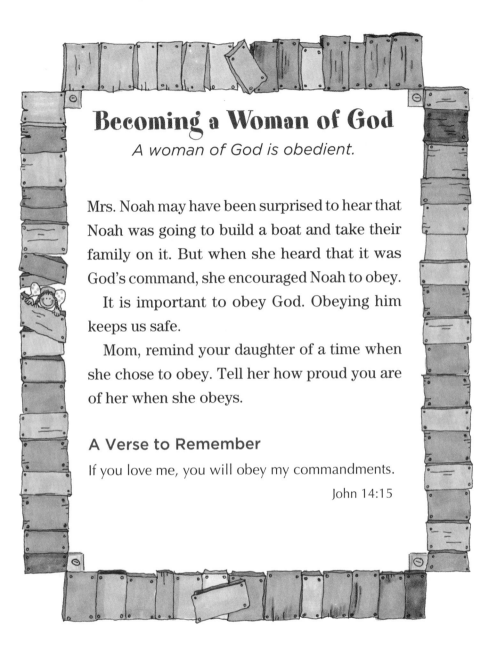

Becoming a Woman of God

A woman of God is obedient.

Mrs. Noah may have been surprised to hear that Noah was going to build a boat and take their family on it. But when she heard that it was God's command, she encouraged Noah to obey.

It is important to obey God. Obeying him keeps us safe.

Mom, remind your daughter of a time when she chose to obey. Tell her how proud you are of her when she obeys.

A Verse to Remember

If you love me, you will obey my commandments.

John 14:15

A Rainbow Promise

Genesis 7–9

At first, the pounding of the rain was like a gentle lullaby. But soon Mrs. Noah noticed the rain was falling harder and harder and the wind was blowing. *That's some storm out there! The whole earth must be covered with water by now,* she thought.

Noah's family and the animals were in the ark for a long, long time. Mrs. Noah stayed busy cleaning up and keeping her family fed and their clothes cleaned.

One morning, days and days after the rain had stopped, the big boat bumped into something. "Ground!" Mrs. Noah shouted. "The flood is going down and we've touched ground!" She peeked out and saw that the ark was sitting on dry ground—the very tip-top of a mountain.

She began packing up things and sweeping up the floor, getting ready to leave the boat. "I can't wait to stand on solid ground again," she cried.

Finally, Noah said it was safe to leave the ark. "Fresh air, blue sky, and sunshine," sang Mrs. Noah. She grabbed Noah's hands and danced with joy.

In the middle of celebrating they noticed the most beautiful rainbow they had ever seen.

"It shows my promise," God said. "I won't ever let a flood destroy the earth again. When you see a rainbow, remember my promise and how much I love you."

"Thank you for your promise," Mr. and Mrs. Noah prayed. "We love you too."

Becoming a Woman of God

*A woman of God is thankful
for God's care.*

When Mr. and Mrs. Noah stepped out of the boat and saw a brand-new, shiny clean world, they thanked God for keeping them safe from the terrible flood and for his wonderful rainbow promise.

Do you remember to thank God for everything he has given you? Mom, pray a thank-you prayer with your little girl right now.

A Verse to Remember

Give thanks to the Lord because he is good,
because his mercy endures forever.

Psalm 107:1

On the Road Again

Genesis 12:1–9

Sarah packed their belongings and Abraham tied the bags onto the camels. Just as she closed the last bag, her best friend came in. "Sarah, you're not really leaving, are you? I'll miss you so much."

"I will miss you too, but God said that we should go—
so we will," Sarah said kindly. "God promised that if we
obey him, he will give us as many descendants as there
are stars in the sky."

We can trust God to keep his promises

Sarah stayed close to Abraham as they left Haran with their servants, the servants' families, and all their animals. Their friends lined the road to say good-bye. Sarah wondered if she would ever see them again.

The caravan moved slowly. They waited for God to lead them where he wanted them to go. "Miss Sarah, will you sing to me while we walk?" a tiny voice asked.

"Of course, little one." Sarah smiled. Soon a large group of children surrounded Sarah, talking with her and listening to her songs about God's love and care.

Sarah sometimes wished they could stay in one place for a while. But she and Abraham were a team, and they tried to always obey God. Deep in Sarah's heart God's promise was still alive—someday they would have children of their own.

Becoming a Woman of God

*A woman of God trusts
in God's promises.*

God promised Abraham and Sarah that they would have as many family members as there were stars in the sky. But when they were old, they didn't have even one child.

Sometimes we have to wait for God's promises to happen. Waiting is hard, but it teaches us to trust God.

When have you waited a long time for something?

A Verse to Remember

Trust the LORD with all your heart,
and do not rely on your own understanding.

Proverbs 3:5

A Dangerous Giggle

Genesis 18:1–15; 21:1–7

Sarah listened from inside the tent as the three strangers talked with Abraham. They promised her ninety-nine-year-old husband that she would have a baby by this same time next year. *How long have we waited for God's promise to come true?* she thought.

Suddenly the thought of her old body carrying a baby struck Sarah as funny. Before she could stop it, a big giggle rolled out of her mouth.

The men sitting outside with Abraham suddenly stopped talking. "Why did Sarah laugh at what we told you?" they asked. "Is anything too hard for God?"

Several months later it was obvious that the men's message had truly been from God. "Abraham, I can barely see my feet anymore!" Sarah said, giggling. "Oh, come quick!" Abraham hurried to Sarah and laid his hand on her stomach. He felt the baby wiggle and kick.

Nearly a year after the visit by the three men, Abraham and Sarah became parents of a baby boy. They named him Isaac, which means laughter. Sarah cradled her precious miracle baby in her arms and whispered, "Praise God for promises kept."

Becoming a Woman of God

A woman of God praises God.

Sarah waited a long time for God to give her a child. When Isaac was born she was very happy. Sarah knew that he was truly a gift from God. What did she do then? She praised God.

God loves to hear the praises of his children because it shows we're thinking about everything he does for us. What can you praise God for today?

A Verse to Remember

I will thank the LORD at all times.
My mouth will always praise him.

Psalm 34:1

My Son, My Son

Genesis 27:1–28:6

Of course Rebekah loved Esau. He was her firstborn son. But her second son, Jacob, was special. So when Rebekah heard Isaac say that he was ready to give the family blessing to Esau, she made a plan.

"I want you to get that blessing!" Rebekah told Jacob. "The one who gets it will lead the family. It must be you! Your father asked Esau to make his favorite meal before receiving the blessing. So bring me two goats and I'll cook a meal. You can take it to your father before Esau returns from hunting and you will get the blessing."

"I'm not sure this is a good idea," Jacob said. But he did what his mother said.

Rebekah cooked, then helped Jacob put goatskins on his arms so his skin would feel hairy like Esau's. He put on Esau's clothes so he would smell like his brother. Then he took the food to his father, who was old and blind and easily confused.

Isaac thought he was talking to Esau. He said, "My beloved son, may God bless you richly, may nations serve you, and may you rule over your brothers."

When Esau came back, he begged Isaac for the blessing, but it was too late. Once the blessing was given, it couldn't be changed! Esau vowed to get even with his brother, so Jacob had to leave home. Rebekah watched him go. "What have I done?" she cried. "Jacob has the blessing—that's what I wanted, but now he is gone."

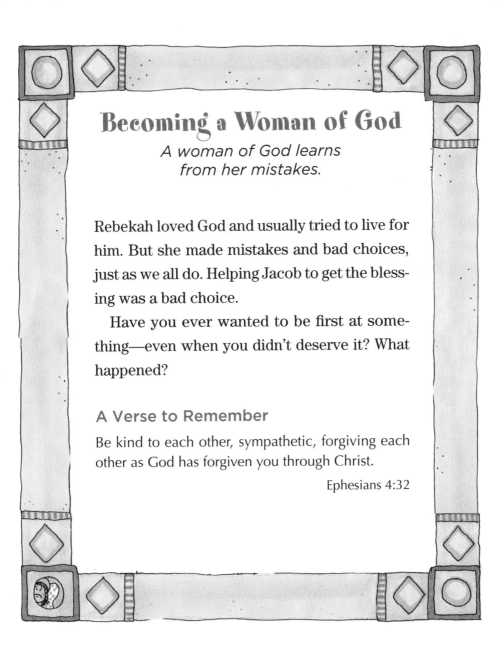

Becoming a Woman of God

*A woman of God learns
from her mistakes.*

Rebekah loved God and usually tried to live for
him. But she made mistakes and bad choices,
just as we all do. Helping Jacob to get the blessing was a bad choice.

Have you ever wanted to be first at something—even when you didn't deserve it? What
happened?

A Verse to Remember

Be kind to each other, sympathetic, forgiving each
other as God has forgiven you through Christ.

Ephesians 4:32

He Loves Me,
He Loves Me Not

Genesis 29:15–30

He loves me, he loves me not. He loves me . . . Rachel plucked petals from a flower as she thought about Jacob, the young man who had come to work for her father.

Jacob certainly seemed to like her too. He looked for ways to be around her every day. Rachel was very happy when Jacob asked her father if he could marry her. Her father, Laban, said Jacob could marry her if he worked for him for seven years first. Jacob was happy to do that.

Sometimes Rachel thought the seven years were flying by. But sometimes she thought they would never end. She just enjoyed having Jacob nearby every day.

But when the wedding day finally came, Rachel was sad because her father had a sneaky plan. "You must marry my older daughter, Leah," Laban told Jacob. "It is our custom for the older daughter to marry first."

Rachel cried and Jacob was angry when he learned it was Leah he must marry, not Rachel. "You can marry Rachel too," Laban said, "but only if you work for me another seven years."

A while later, Laban allowed Jacob to marry Rachel. But Jacob worked for Laban another seven years.

Becoming a Woman of God

A woman of God learns that other people make choices that affect her life.

Rachel had no control over her father's choices. All she knew was that she wanted to marry Jacob.

Sometimes things do not go the way you think they should.

But remember that nothing surprises God. Nothing happens that he doesn't know about first.

When was a time that your plans were changed because of someone else?

A Verse to Remember

Blessed is the person who trusts the LORD.
The LORD will be his confidence.

Jeremiah 17:7

The Riverboat Bed

Exodus 2:1–10

"I don't care what Pharaoh ordered. I know God has wonderful plans for my son!" Jochebed said. She hugged her little baby, promising herself to protect him from Pharaoh's soldiers—even though they had orders to get rid of all Hebrew baby boys.

"Miriam, keep the baby quiet. Sing to him," she said to her daughter. For three months Jochebed managed to keep her precious boy a secret, but now his cries were getting stronger.

"Mother, how much longer can we hide him? Sooner or later someone will report to the soldiers that we have a baby here," Miriam whispered.

"I won't let them take my son. Go to the river and pick some reeds for me. I have a plan," Jochebed said. She worked quickly, weaving reeds to make a small basket, then covering it with tar.

Jochebed held her son close, feeling his soft skin and enjoying his baby smell. Then she laid him in the basket. She carried the little basket down to the river and set it afloat. "Miriam, stay here and keep watch," Jochebed whispered as tears ran down her cheeks. "Please, God, take care of my baby," she prayed.

Jochebed waited for Miriam's report. Finally Miriam burst into the room. "Pharaoh's daughter found the baby," she said excitedly. "She's going to keep him, but she needs help taking care of him. Come quick! You can get the job!"

"I praise you, God," Jochebed prayed, "for taking care of my son!"

Becoming a Woman of God

A woman of God is active.

More than anything, Jochebed wanted her son to live. So she did what she could and God did the rest. He took care of Moses.

When you believe that something needs to be done, ask God for his help and wisdom, and then get moving!

When have you helped work on something that needed to be done?

A Verse to Remember

Lead me in your truth and teach me
because you are God, my savior.
I wait all day long for you.

Psalm 25:5

If God Says Go,
Then We Go

Exodus 3:1–4:17

When Moses came from Egypt, Zipporah fell in love
with the kind stranger. After they got married, Moses
worked as a shepherd for her father.

One day Moses came home with surprising news. "I was out in the fields with the sheep and I heard a voice. Believe it or not the voice was coming from a bush—a bush was talking to me! And not just any bush—a bush that was on fire. It burned and burned, but it didn't burn up!"

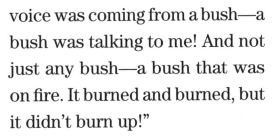

"A bush talked to you?" Zipporah asked in disbelief, trying to understand his story.

"It was God's voice speaking from the burning bush. He asked me to do a special job for him."

At first Zipporah couldn't believe it, but then she became sure that it was God speaking to Moses. She was very proud of Moses. *God asked my Moses to lead the Israelites out of Egypt*, she thought.

Zipporah worried as she began packing for the trip to Egypt. "I believe Moses can do anything he sets his mind to, but God had to talk him into doing this job. At least his brother Aaron can come along to be his helper. Moses will feel better if he's not alone."

Moses and Zipporah said good-bye to her family. All
during the long trip to Egypt, she wondered what the
future held. Would Pharaoh let the Israelites leave just
because Moses asked him to? "Dear God," she prayed,
"help Moses. Please guide his every move."

Becoming a Woman of God

A woman of God prays for her family.

The most important thing Zipporah could do for Moses was pray for him. He was really going to need God's help!

Are there people you pray for every day? Is someone praying for you every day?

A Verse to Remember

However, if my people, who are called by my name, will humble themselves, pray, search for me, and turn from their evil ways, then I will hear their prayer from heaven, forgive their sins, and heal their country.

2 Chronicles 7:14

My Brother's Keeper

Exodus 7:1–10:29

Miriam wiggled through the crowd. She wanted to hear everything that was being said. The angry people were shouting at her brother, "Why did you come here? Since you asked Pharaoh to let us leave Egypt, he's just made us work harder!" Miriam sighed. She longed to take care of her brother like she had done when he was young.

Moses was only doing what God told him to do and yet the people were so angry. "Trust God," Moses told them. "He wants to free you from slavery!" But the people would not listen.

God is going to have to do something big to convince these people, Miriam thought.

Of course God did do something big when he made all the water in Egypt turn to blood.

The Egyptians panicked. "What will we drink?" they asked.

God did it, Miriam thought. *Now the Egyptians will know that he is boss!*

But Pharaoh refused to let the Israelites leave.

Each time Moses asked and each time Pharaoh refused to let the people leave, something awful happened to the Egyptians. Frogs filled the land, and gnats bugged the Egyptians, then hail killed their crops. On and on it went until nine terrible things had happened to the Egyptians.

But Pharaoh was stubborn. He would not let the Israel-ites leave. Miriam was amazed at her brother's complete trust in God. She wondered what God's amazing power would do next to get Pharaoh's attention.

♥ Trust in God ♥

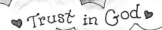

Becoming a Woman of God

A woman of God recognizes his power.

Miriam knew that it was God who was making terrible things happen to the Egyptians. God showed them his amazing power, but still Pharaoh would not obey him.

Mom, talk with your daughter about some ways that you see God's power today. Thank him for his power, strength, and love for you.

A Verse to Remember

O LORD, our Lord, how majestic is your name throughout the earth!

Psalm 8:9

Saving the Worst for Last

Exodus 11:1–15:21

Miriam hugged her oldest child as she watched her husband paint the door frame of their house with lamb's blood. "Moses says this will keep us safe from the last plague. The firstborn son in every Egyptian home will die tonight," he said. A lump rose in Miriam's throat at the thought. *Why hadn't Pharaoh just listened to Moses?*

That night hundreds of
Egyptian children died—
even Pharaoh's son. Through
his tears, Pharaoh finally told Moses,
"Get out of Egypt."

A huge cloud led the Israelites out of
Egypt. God was in the cloud, so the Israelites knew he was leading them.

After they had walked many miles, Moses said they should set up camp near the Red Sea. Later, Miriam was making dinner when she heard shouting. Panic gripped her heart when she saw a cloud of dust in the distance. Pharaoh had changed his mind about letting them go. His army was chasing them!

"Watch what God will do for you!" Moses shouted. Miriam held her breath as her brother climbed onto a rock and held his staff over the Red Sea. Suddenly, the waters rolled apart and piled up into two big walls.

The Israelites walked through the sea on dry ground. As the last Israelite came through, the Egyptians raced in after them. But the water crashed down on the soldiers. Miriam grabbed a tambourine and sang with joy, "Praise the Lord for a wonderful victory!"

Becoming a Woman of God

*A woman of God
looks for God's bigger plan.*

Miriam knew that God had sent plagues on Egypt. When the Egyptians had the Israelites trapped, she saw God rescue them again. Miriam could see God's plan for her people unfolding.

Mom, talk with your daughter about how you see his plan unfolding in your lives. How does he take care of you?

A Verse to Remember

Shout happily to the LORD, all the earth.
Serve the LORD cheerfully.
Come into his presence with a joyful song.

Psalm 100:1–2

Eating Out

Exodus 16

Everywhere the Hebrew woman went she heard people complaining. "Why did Moses drag us out to this desert? At least in Egypt we had food to eat." The woman sighed. "I'm hungry too. And it's hard to hear my children cry that they're hungry when I have nothing to give them."

She went along to listen when the people asked Moses what he was going to do about their problems. She was surprised to hear Moses say, "God has heard your cries. Every morning he will give you food from heaven, and every evening he will send you meat." She wondered what that meant.

Later that day, the woman heard a strange noise. Peeking out of her tent, she saw hundreds, maybe thousands of birds on the ground. People grabbed them and rushed to cook and eat them. *Wow*, she thought, *this is just like Moses said.*

For the first night in a very long time, the woman and her children went to bed with full tummies. *God is so good*, she thought. The next morning, she was as surprised as everyone else when she saw white flakes covering the ground.

"What is it?" the woman asked.

"Manna," someone answered. "It's God's gift of food to us."

She bit into the crunchy white wafer. *God's gift of food from heaven—so this is what Moses meant.* "Thank you, God, for taking care of us!" she prayed.

Becoming a Woman of God

*A woman of God
knows God meets her daily needs.*

The Hebrew woman learned that God cared about all her needs. She was hungry and God helped her.

How does God take care of you every day? Think about all the things you need from the time you wake up each morning until you go to bed at night. Thank God for his daily care.

A Verse to Remember

It is good to give thanks to the LORD,
to make music to praise your name, O Most High.

Psalm 92:1

The Perfect Ten

Exodus 18:5; 19:1–20:21

I'm so tired, Zipporah thought. Since Moses had led them out of Egypt the Israelites had walked for days and days. Now they were camped right at the base of Mount Sinai, and Zipporah just wanted to rest.

Moses came in just as Zipporah was lying down for a short nap. "I'm going up on the mountain," he told her.

"Now? We just got settled. Can't you rest for a while?"

"I am tired, but God called me, so I must go," Moses said.

When Moses came back, he announced that God wanted him to give a message to all the people. Three days later, Zipporah's heart was pounding as she stood with the other Israelites at the base of Mount Sinai. Thunder and lightning crashed on the mountain and a thick dark cloud covered it.

Zipporah was more impressed than ever with Moses's courage. People around her shook and trembled in fear as Moses disappeared into the cloud to speak with God all by himself.

Days later Zipporah prayed, "God, I know you are protecting him, but he has been gone a long time. I'm starting to get worried about him."

When Moses did return, Zipporah was surprised to see that Moses was holding two slabs of stone. "They're rules," he told her. "God wrote ten rules for the people to live by."

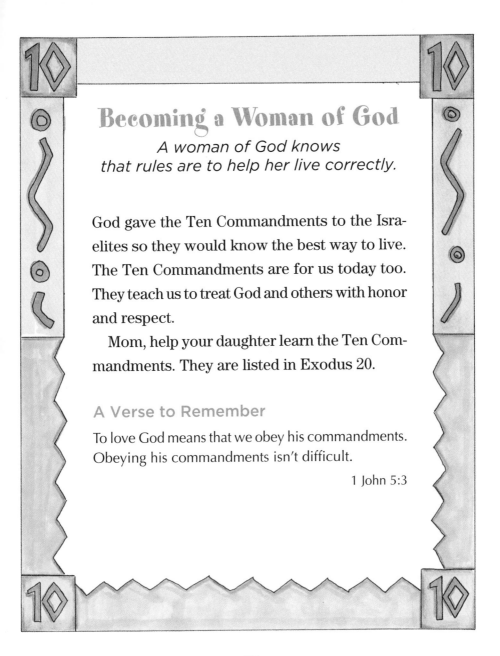

Becoming a Woman of God

*A woman of God knows
that rules are to help her live correctly.*

God gave the Ten Commandments to the Israelites so they would know the best way to live. The Ten Commandments are for us today too. They teach us to treat God and others with honor and respect.

Mom, help your daughter learn the Ten Commandments. They are listed in Exodus 20.

A Verse to Remember

To love God means that we obey his commandments. Obeying his commandments isn't difficult.

1 John 5:3

The Walls Fall Down

Joshua 2, 6

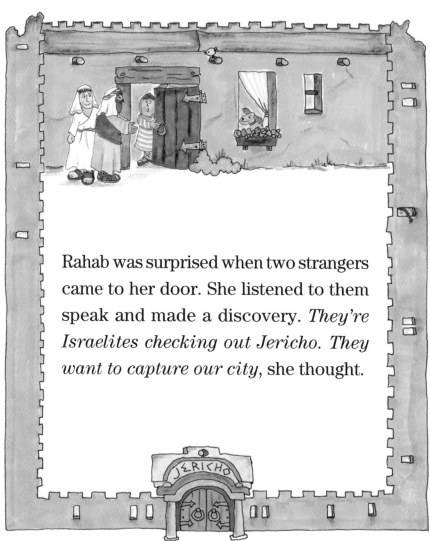

Rahab was surprised when two strangers came to her door. She listened to them speak and made a discovery. *They're Israelites checking out Jericho. They want to capture our city*, she thought.

Rahab knew how powerful the Israelite God was. So when soldiers came looking for the spies, she made a quick decision. "Hide on the roof. I'll get rid of the soldiers," she told the two men.

After the soldiers left, she told the spies, "I risked my life to save you. Will you protect me when you capture the city?" The spies said yes and gave her a red rope to hang in her window so they could find her quickly.

The Israelite army arrived a few weeks later. Rahab packed her things and waited to be rescued. But for six days the Israelites just silently marched around the city—once a day. *Why don't they just attack?* Rahab wondered.

On the seventh day the Israelites began their daily march. But they didn't stop after marching once around the city. They marched around and around. Then, the priests blew their horns and the Israelites shouted. The huge walls around Jericho began to crumble and fall.

Rahab fell to her knees and prayed, "O God, please let the spies remember their promise." Just then a soldier grabbed her arm.

"Are you Rahab?" he asked. She nodded and he said, "Come on, I'll help you get out of here."

They remembered! "Thank you, God," Rahab prayed. "You are an awesome God."

Becoming a Woman of God

*A woman of God chooses God even
when those around her do not.*

When the spies first came to Jericho, Rahab
respected God's power and chose to let that
power protect her instead of destroy her.

How can you gently show others that obeying God is important to you?

A Verse to Remember

Israel, what does the LORD your God want you to
do? He wants you to fear him, follow all his directions, love him, and worship him with all your
heart and with all your soul.

Deuteronomy 10:12

A Woman Shall Lead Them

Judges 4–5

How many times will God have to rescue my people from their foolish choices? Deborah wondered. The Israelites had often turned away from God and then begged for his help when they were in trouble.

Deborah was a prophetess. She gave God's word to the people. It was a big job, especially because the people never remembered to obey God's words for very long. Then one day God told Deborah his plan for freeing the Israelites from the evil King Jabin who was making them prisoners.

Deborah immediately told Barak, "God says to take your army to Mount Tabor. God will bring Sisera, Jabin's army commander there. You can capture him!" Deborah said.

Barak's response shocked her: "I will go only if you go with me!"

"What?" Deborah shouted. "If I come, then a woman will get the credit for this victory, not you!"

Barak didn't care. He wanted Deborah with him.

So Deborah and Barak marched up Mount Tabor with ten thousand men. Deborah waited for Barak to command his army to attack, but he didn't. "Go on!" she finally shouted. "God brought Sisera to you. Capture him!"

Deborah's words pushed Barak into action and the battle began. But Sisera ran away. Just as Deborah had predicted, the honor of defeating Sisera and freeing the Israelite people went to a woman. A woman named Jael attacked Sisera while he was sleeping. Deborah celebrated the victory with a song of praise to God!

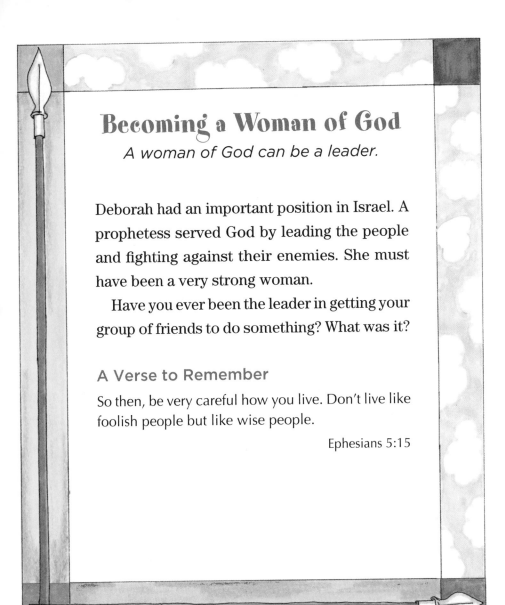

Becoming a Woman of God

A woman of God can be a leader.

Deborah had an important position in Israel. A prophetess served God by leading the people and fighting against their enemies. She must have been a very strong woman.

Have you ever been the leader in getting your group of friends to do something? What was it?

A Verse to Remember

So then, be very careful how you live. Don't live like foolish people but like wise people.

Ephesians 5:15

A Foreigner
in a Foreign Land

Ruth 1-4

Ruth's husband was from another country. He was a nice man whose family had moved to Moab because there was no food in their homeland. His mother, Naomi, was kind to Ruth and her other daughter-in-law, Orpah.

Ruth loved her husband and was very happy. Then one dark day everything changed. Ruth's and Orpah's husbands died. Ruth, Orpah, and Naomi were sad and hugged each other and cried.

One day Naomi decided to return to her homeland of Judah. "I won't let you go alone," Ruth said. Orpah went along too.

But soon after they began the trip, Naomi said, "Go home, girls. You're young. You can marry again. Go home to your people." Orpah went back home, but Ruth stayed with Naomi.

When Ruth and Naomi arrived in Judah, they did not have jobs or money. Ruth went to a grain field that belonged to a man named Boaz. She picked up any grain left on the ground by the workers. She and Naomi made it into bread so they had food to eat.

"Boaz is a nice man who treats his workers kindly,"
Ruth reported to Naomi.

"Ruth works hard and is very loyal to Naomi," Boaz's
friends told him. Soon Boaz and Ruth were married.
They had a baby boy and named him Obed.

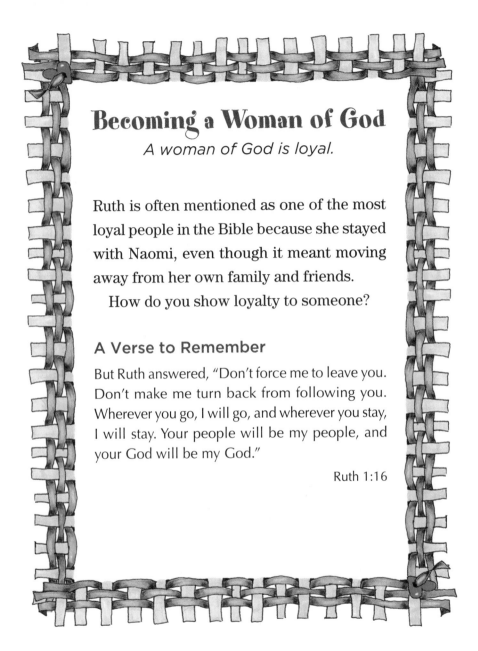

Becoming a Woman of God

A woman of God is loyal.

Ruth is often mentioned as one of the most loyal people in the Bible because she stayed with Naomi, even though it meant moving away from her own family and friends.

How do you show loyalty to someone?

A Verse to Remember

But Ruth answered, "Don't force me to leave you. Don't make me turn back from following you. Wherever you go, I will go, and wherever you stay, I will stay. Your people will be my people, and your God will be my God."

Ruth 1:16

The Shame of Shames

1 Samuel 1

Peninnah never missed a chance to brag that she had lots of children while Hannah had none.

Elkanah tried to encourage his wife. "Hannah, I love you. It doesn't matter to me that we have no children." But Hannah was still sad. She really wanted to be a mother.

One year, Elkanah and Hannah went to Shiloh to worship God at the temple. Hannah was sad and could think of only one thing to pray. "Please, God," she cried. "I promise that if you will bless me with a child, I will give him back to you, to serve you."

Eli, the priest, was watching Hannah pray at the altar. Her lips were moving, but she wasn't making any sound. Eli didn't know the sadness in Hannah's heart or the pain in her prayer.

Hannah explained to Eli, "I have been pouring out my heart, begging God to give me a baby."

"Go in peace," Eli replied, "and may God grant your prayer."

A while later Hannah did have a baby boy. She named him Samuel, which means, "Because I asked the Lord for him." Hannah remembered her promise to God; so when Samuel was old enough, she took him to live with Eli at the temple where he would learn to serve God.

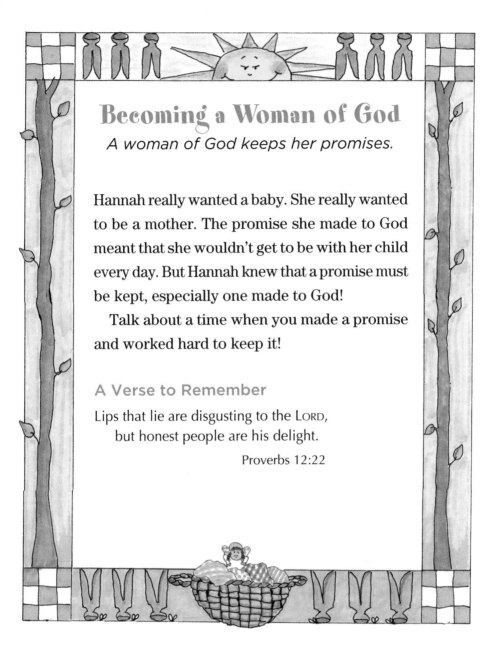

Becoming a Woman of God

A woman of God keeps her promises.

Hannah really wanted a baby. She really wanted to be a mother. The promise she made to God meant that she wouldn't get to be with her child every day. But Hannah knew that a promise must be kept, especially one made to God!

Talk about a time when you made a promise and worked hard to keep it!

A Verse to Remember

Lips that lie are disgusting to the LORD,
but honest people are his delight.

Proverbs 12:22

The Peacemaker

1 Samuel 25:1–35

"Nabal makes people so angry!" Abigail said to herself. She tossed food into baskets as quickly as her hands would move. She was right. Her husband, Nabal, was mean to everyone. And this time he had gone too far.

"I don't know if I can help him out of this trouble. He made King David angry. Everyone knows about David—we sing songs about his amazing victories. He's our hero!

"All David wanted was a little food. It wouldn't have been hard for Nabal to give him food for his soldiers. We have plenty. But no—instead Nabal insulted David. Oh my, David is so angry!"

After Abigail finished packing food, she carried the baskets outside and tied them on donkeys. Then she headed down the dusty road toward David's camp.

A few minutes later, she looked up and saw David and his men coming up the hill—on their way to attack her husband.

When David got closer, Abigail called out, "Sir, I accept responsibility for what Nabal did. I didn't know about your request until it was too late, so I've brought you some food now. Don't harm my husband; please forgive him," Abigail begged.

Abigail breathed a sigh of relief when David thanked her for stopping him from doing something wrong. She went home praising God that David had heard her request.

Becoming a Woman of God

A woman of God is a peacemaker.

Abigail knew that her husband was in trouble. She came up with a plan and went out of her way to make peace with King David.

How do you feel when you are around people who are fighting? It's not much fun, is it? Have you ever tried to be a peacemaker and asked your friends or family members to make up?

A Verse to Remember

See how good and pleasant it is
　　when brothers and sisters live together in harmony!

Psalm 133:1

Elijah's Bread Recipe

1 Kings 17:8-16

The woman had skipped meals for days so her son would have food to eat. She remembered when her husband was alive and they had lots of food.

Suddenly a man's voice surprised her. "Excuse me, could I have a drink of water?" She looked up to see Elijah, a prophet of God. She laid down the sticks she had been gathering and went to get water. "I could use a bite of bread too," Elijah added. The woman choked back tears because she couldn't help him.

She looked over at her precious son. "I wish I could help you," she whispered to Elijah. "But there isn't a piece of bread left in my house. I was just gathering sticks to cook up the little bit of flour and oil I have left into a small loaf of bread. When that's gone, my son and I will have nothing to eat."

Elijah said, "Don't worry. Go ahead and bake your loaf of bread. But make a small one for me first. You'll have plenty of flour and oil." The woman didn't understand but she didn't argue.

After she had baked a small loaf for Elijah the woman was amazed that there was still flour and oil left in her jars. She made bread for herself and her son and again flour and oil were left over. The woman praised God because her flour and oil never ran out. "God is good. He has taken care of us!" she exclaimed.

Becoming a Woman of God

*A woman of God believes
God has a plan.*

The woman in this story did what Elijah asked, even though she knew that she was out of food. God blessed her obedience.

Sometimes it's hard to do what you're asked to do if you can't see the end result.

Mom, talk with your daughter about a time you followed God's plan when you didn't know what would happen.

A Verse to Remember

The LORD is my shepherd.
I am never in need.

Psalm 23:1

Elisha's Room

2 Kings 4:8-11

The woman from the little town of Shunem made sure that her house was always neat and clean. Everyone in Shunem knew that the woman was very kind and generous.

The gentle woman was a good cook and generous hostess. The first time Elisha came to town she invited him to stay at her home. She enjoyed having him as a guest. After all, he was a prophet of God. She gave him a nice room and delicious food.

After one of Elisha's visits, the woman was cleaning the guest room when an idea popped into her mind. Later that night she shared it with her husband. "Why don't we build a room that will be just for Elisha? Then anytime he is in town he will know that he has a place to stay."

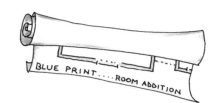

The woman's husband was surprised by her suggestion, but he was happy to do it. The room was built and furnished before Elisha came back to town.

Thank You, God

When Elisha knocked on her door a few weeks later, the woman welcomed him inside. She led him through the house. "We have a surprise for you, Elisha. Look what we've made for you," she said. Elisha was very happy. He thanked God for the kind woman and her generous husband.

Becoming a Woman of God

A woman of God is generous.

The kind woman in Shunem generously shared what she had to help Elisha. God is pleased when we share what he gives us, especially when we use our belongings to help his workers.

When have you shared something with someone else? In what ways can you share with others now?

A Verse to Remember

People should be concerned about others and not just about themselves.

1 Corinthians 10:24

Good Advice
for Naaman

2 Kings 5:1–19

Mrs. Naaman was kind to the little girl. She knew the girl missed her mother very much so she treated her nicely.

The little girl worked hard for Mrs. Naaman and did her work well. One day the little girl saw Mrs. Naaman crying. "Why are you crying?" she asked. The woman seemed very upset.

"I'm crying because my husband is sick. He has to leave home and live in a special place outside of town. I'm going to miss him very much."

The little girl was sad. She liked Mr. Naaman too. So she bravely said, "He doesn't have to be sick. He can go see God's prophet, Elisha. I'm sure Elisha could help him."

The little girl was sure that God would help Elisha heal Naaman. So Mrs. Naaman told her husband to visit the prophet. But on the way Elisha's servant met him and said, "Elisha says you should go wash in the Jordan River seven times." Naaman was angry that Elisha didn't talk with him in person, so he decided to just go home.

Back at Naaman's house the little girl prayed with all her heart that Mr. Naaman would see God's power. When Naaman finally did obey Elisha and was healed, the little girl danced with joy! She had helped the Naamans in two ways: Mr. Naaman was healed, and both Mr. and Mrs. Naaman knew that God's power had healed him.

Becoming a Woman of God

A woman of God can be a child.

This story shows that even a child can lead people to God. The girl's faith in God was so strong that she knew God could heal Naaman.

Who told you about God's love? Can you think of ways to share God's love with others?

A Verse to Remember

Don't let anyone look down on you for being young. Instead, make your speech, behavior, love, faith, and purity an example for other believers.

1 Timothy 4:12

Esther Wins a Beauty Contest

Esther 1-10

"Esther, please help us. This may be the very reason God made you queen." Esther didn't want to hear what Mordecai was saying. She was just a teenager when she was chosen from hundreds of girls and made queen of Persia. But now the young queen faced a problem.

The problem started because Haman, a government leader, wanted everyone to bow down to him. One Jewish man, Esther's cousin, Mordecai, refused to bow. He said he would bow only to God. Now Haman wanted to make a law that would get rid of all the Jews!

"I can't help. No one, not even the king, knows that I am Jewish. It was your idea for me to keep that a secret," Esther said to Mordecai.

"I know, but all of us—including you—are in danger if we don't think of some way to stop Haman," Mordecai said.

Esther wondered what the king would say when he found out she was Jewish. Esther gathered her courage and sent a note to Mordecai. *I'm going to talk to the king. Pray for me.*

Esther invited the king and Haman to a special dinner. They enjoyed the food and were laughing and talking when Esther found the courage to say, "Haman is planning to get rid of me and my relatives!"

Esther explained Haman's whole plan. She breathed a sigh of relief when the king ordered that Haman be arrested. The Jewish people were saved, thanks to the courage of a beautiful, brave queen.

Becoming a Woman of God
A woman of God takes a stand for him.

Wasn't Queen Esther brave? Even if she was very scared, she knew she had to stop Haman.

Have you ever heard someone saying mean things about someone else? Did you try to stop them? It's not easy to be brave, is it? Sometimes obeying God means being brave.

A Verse to Remember

I can do everything through Christ who strengthens me.

Philippians 4:13

We're Having a Baby

Luke 1:5–25, 57–64

Elizabeth shook her head in frustration. "What are you trying to tell me? Why don't you just talk?"

Her husband, Zechariah, was just as frustrated as she was. Finally, he picked up a stick and wrote in the dirt, "We're going to have a baby."

"A baby?" she cried. "Do you know how old I am?"

Zechariah quickly scribbled another word in the dust: Angel. Through his scribbles Elizabeth learned that an angel had told her husband that they would have a baby boy and that they must name him John.

Their son would prepare the world for the coming Savior. She also found out why Zechariah was drawing signs in the dust instead of telling her this news. He doubted the angel's message so the messenger from God had taken his voice away until the baby was born. After hearing that, Elizabeth was careful not to question any of Zechariah's news.

Sometimes Elizabeth would rub her hand across her stomach and think, *A baby. I'm going to have a baby.* She and Zechariah had prayed for a child for many years. She was so happy.

Nine months later, friends and relatives gathered with Zechariah and Elizabeth to celebrate the birth of their son. Elizabeth cradled the child in her arms. Everyone wondered what the baby's name would be. Zechariah held up a tablet in the air with four words scratched on it: "His name is John." Suddenly he was able to talk again, and he began to praise God.

Becoming a Woman of God

A woman of God enjoys God's surprises.

Elizabeth and Zechariah must have thought their lives were all settled. They were old and had no children.

Then God gave them a special surprise! He gave them a baby in their old age. When God is involved, nothing is impossible!

What surprises has God given you?

A Verse to Remember

Ask, and you will receive. Search, and you will find. Knock, and the door will be opened for you.

Matthew 7:7

Big News for Mary

Luke 1:26–38

Mary dragged the heavy wooden bucket into the house. The daily trip to the town well for the family's water was tiring. Sitting down to rest, Mary thought drifted to wedding plans and her fiancé, Joseph.

I'd better get back to work, Mary thought. Suddenly she realized that she wasn't alone.

"Hello, Mary," a stranger said. "Congratulations; you are blessed. God is with you." Mary knew then that the stranger was an angel sent from God.

"Don't be afraid, Mary. I've come to tell you that you are going to have a baby," the angel said.

"I can't have a baby," she whispered. "I'm not even married."

"Your baby will be God's Son," the angel said. "God says to name him Jesus. His kingdom will never end!"

Mary had never felt so confused, or frightened, or honored. What would Joseph say? What would her family say? Had God really chosen her?

As Mary stared into the angel's face, he reminded her, "Nothing is impossible with God, Mary."

Mary closed her eyes and took a deep breath before saying, "I am God's servant. I will do whatever he wants me to do!" When she opened her eyes, the angel was gone.

Becoming a Woman of God

A woman of God is chosen by God.

Mary was chosen for a great honor. But God didn't choose her because of anything she did. He chose her because she loved God and wanted to please him.

Being chosen makes us feel good. Have you ever been chosen for something special?

A Verse to Remember

The Spirit himself testifies with our spirit that we are God's children.

Romans 8:16

A Promise Is Born

Luke 2:1–21

Going on a bumpy donkey ride was the last thing Mary should be doing. Her baby would be born any day. *If only we didn't have to go to Bethlehem for the census,* she thought.

"Are you all right, Mary?" Joseph asked. She told him she was fine, but the baby seemed to kick harder with every step the donkey took.

"Hang on, Mary, we're almost there. We'll find a room in Bethlehem," Joseph promised.

When they arrived in Bethlehem, Mary waited while Joseph looked for a place to stay, but he returned with bad news.

"There are no more rooms. The innkeeper says the whole town is full. But since you're pregnant he said we could stay in his stable," Joseph said.

Mary slid from the donkey to the mound of straw Joseph had gathered and fell asleep. Sometime after dark Mary woke up. "Joseph, wake up. The baby!"

Joseph tried to comfort her. But it was only when he laid the baby in her arms that Mary relaxed and thanked God for this incredible miracle.

Mary was filled with love for her baby, yet she barely dared to think about who he really was. Then she looked up to see some shepherds peeking over the stable door. "An angel told us our Savior was born," they said. Their words swam in Mary's mind. Softly, she began to sing, "My baby, my Savior . . . I'm holding Jesus in my arms."

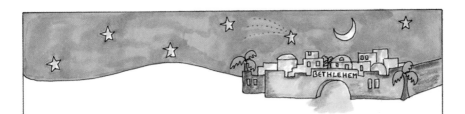

Becoming a Woman of God

A woman of God does the work of God.

The work that Mary did for God was a great honor, but it was also difficult. Sometimes God's work is challenging, but the end result is wonderful and exciting. Doing God's work gives us great joy.

Do you have chores to do? Are some jobs hard? What kind of work do you enjoy doing?

A Verse to Remember

Whatever you do, do it wholeheartedly as though you were working for your real master and not merely for humans.

Colossians 3:23

My Dream Comes True

Luke 2:25–38

Anna loved God so much. She usually spent most of the day kneeling on the hard floor in the temple, praying to him.

One day Anna got up to go check on her old friend, Simeon. She could hear him shouting. To Anna's old ears it sounded as if he were saying, "Praise God! Now I can die a happy man." Anna knew that Simeon was a man of God. What on earth was he shouting about?

Anna shuffled through the temple toward Simeon's voice. Then she saw him holding a baby in his arms. He was shouting, "Praise you, Lord. Just as you promised, I have seen the Savior of Israel, a light for the world! Now I can die a happy man."

Anna crept closer as Simeon gave the child back to his mother. *They must be here to dedicate the baby to God,* Anna thought. Just then she caught a glimpse of the baby's face. At that very moment God showed her that this baby was the Savior that her people were waiting for.

Joy bubbled from deep inside Anna: "Thank you, God, for hearing the prayers of your people. Hallelujah!" Anna stopped every person she met and told them about the child. "The Savior has come. God has heard our prayers! Hallelujah!"

Becoming a Woman of God

A woman of God recognizes her Savior.

When Anna saw baby Jesus, she immediately knew that he was her Savior. Her heart was so close to God that she understood who this little baby was and what he would do when he grew up.

A Verse to Remember

My sheep respond to my voice, and I know who they are. They follow me, and I give them eternal life. They will never be lost, and no one will tear them away from me.

John 10:27–28

Wise Men from the East

Matthew 2:9–12

Nearly two years had passed since Mary and Joseph came to Bethlehem. *Where does the time go?* Mary wondered as she washed clothes. Jesus was a good baby, but even good babies are a lot of work.

Mary glanced at Jesus playing by himself on his blanket. She let her mind wander back to what the angel said about him when he came to tell her she was going to have a baby. She remembered the shepherds' words on the night Jesus was born, and the words of Simeon and Anna in the temple. Sometimes Mary wondered, *What is ahead for this sweet little child?*

Mary had friends in Bethlehem, but she didn't talk with them about who Jesus really was. After all, Jesus looked and acted like a normal two-year-old. Mary didn't know what was going to happen in the future.

One day some men wearing fancy clothes rode their camels right up to Mary and Joseph's little house. "We've come to worship the newborn king," they announced.

How did they find us? Mary wondered. One man answered her unspoken question. "The star led us to you," he said, as he pointed to the bright star in the sky right over her house. The men knelt before Jesus and gave him gifts they had brought. The men worshiped Jesus, and Mary's heart filled with joy.

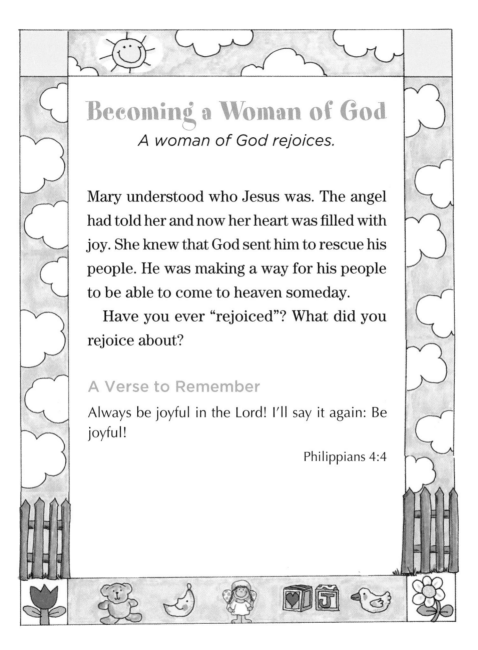

Becoming a Woman of God

A woman of God rejoices.

Mary understood who Jesus was. The angel had told her and now her heart was filled with joy. She knew that God sent him to rescue his people. He was making a way for his people to be able to come to heaven someday.

Have you ever "rejoiced"? What did you rejoice about?

A Verse to Remember

Always be joyful in the Lord! I'll say it again: Be joyful!

Philippians 4:4

My Son Is Lost

Luke 2:41–52

Mary's side hurt, but she kept running. Joseph was ahead of her as they raced back to Jerusalem. *How could we leave Jesus behind?* Mary thought. *He's only twelve years old.*

"Joseph, this was supposed to be a happy time; it's the Passover. What if we can't find him?" Mary cried to her husband.

Joseph waited for her to catch up with him. He hugged her tightly and said, "Trust God, Mary."

Mary and Joseph ran up and down the streets of Jerusalem, stopping people, describing Jesus. "Have you seen him? Please, help us." No one had seen him.

Three days later Mary was exhausted. They still had not found Jesus. "Let's go to the temple and pray for God's help," Joseph suggested. Mary went along and she tried to pray, but the temple was buzzing with people talking about an amazing child who was actually teaching the teachers about God!

A child! It had to be Jesus! Mary's heart filled with relief when she saw Jesus. She said, "We looked everywhere for you. Why did you do this?"

Jesus was puzzled. "Why were you worried? Didn't you know that I would be in my Father's house?" Jesus went home with his parents then. Mary couldn't stop touching his shoulder or brushing his hair back. She was thrilled that he was safe.

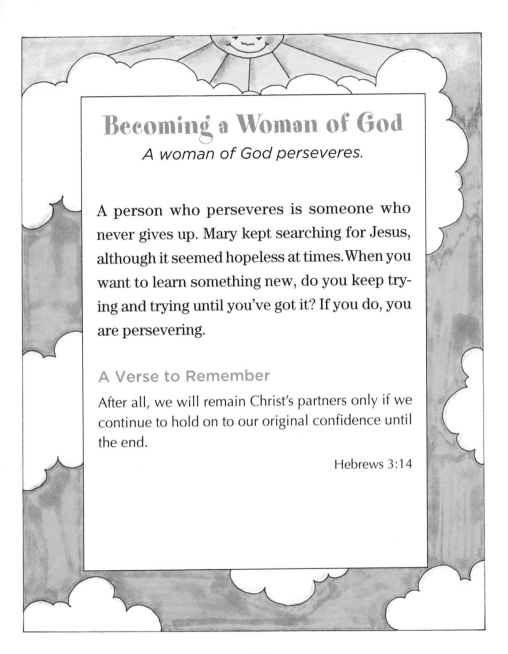

Becoming a Woman of God

A woman of God perseveres.

A person who perseveres is someone who never gives up. Mary kept searching for Jesus, although it seemed hopeless at times. When you want to learn something new, do you keep trying and trying until you've got it? If you do, you are persevering.

A Verse to Remember

After all, we will remain Christ's partners only if we continue to hold on to our original confidence until the end.

Hebrews 3:14

An Unusual Wedding Gift

John 2:1–11

"I love weddings," Mary said to herself. "It's fun to see old friends and family members. The bride always looks so beautiful and the groom is so handsome."

The wedding was as beautiful as Mary had expected.
She was enjoying the party and talking with her friends
until she overheard the master of ceremonies talking
about a problem. Right away Mary knew who could help.

"Jesus, the party isn't over yet, but they've run out of
wine," she said to her son.

Jesus calmly answered, "I can't help."

"It's not the right time for me to do miracles yet," he continued. Mary stared at him with that look only a mother can give. Then she turned to some servants standing nearby. "Do whatever this man tells you to do," she said to them.

Jesus told the servants to fill six big jars with water.

Mary watched to see what would happen. The servants filled the jars and brought them back, but Jesus didn't even touch them. He said, "Take some to the master of ceremonies."

"This is delicious," the man said. "It's the best wine I've ever tasted." The servants were amazed. They knew they had put water into the jars, not wine.

Mary looked around for Jesus. He had disappeared into the crowd after performing a miracle. It was the first of many miracles he would do. His disciples were talking excitedly among themselves. They understood now that Jesus was the Son of God.

THE WHOLE WORLD WILL KNOW HIM

Becoming a Woman of God

A woman of God expects great things.

Mary believed that Jesus could do wonderful miracles. She expected him to help the wedding party by doing a miracle. Jesus saw her faith and did his first miracle.

When you pray, do you expect Jesus to answer? Can you think of a specific prayer you prayed that Jesus answered?

A Verse to Remember

When you ask for something, don't have any doubts. A person who has doubts is like a wave that is blown by the wind and tossed by the sea.

James 1:6

The Woman at the Well

John 4:1-42

Through the years the woman had made bad choices that left her feeling hopeless. She had not felt loved for a long time. She made her daily trip to the well alone. No one walked with her.

As she came close to the well one day she noticed a man standing there. She didn't want to talk to him. She thought he would probably make fun of her. So she went around the well and lowered her bucket into the water. Just then the man asked her for a drink of water.

"I can't believe you're speaking to me, a lowly Samaritan," she said. The woman didn't know that this man was Jesus. But Jesus showed her that he knew many things about her life. At first that scared her and she wanted to run away.

"God loves you," Jesus said quietly. "He wants your love."

"He can't love me; I've done so many bad things," the woman whispered. "I don't understand God. When the Messiah comes maybe he can explain it to me."

Jesus gently said, "I am the Messiah."

The woman ran back to town shouting at the top of her lungs, "I met the Messiah!" Water splashed from her bucket as she grabbed people's arms saying, "Come with me; I want you to meet him too!" Many people believed in Jesus that day because the woman shared the good news she had heard.

Becoming a Woman of God

A woman of God shares the good news.

When the woman met Jesus, she wanted to tell everyone. She wanted everyone in town to meet him, so she called for people to come with her to meet Jesus.

When you have really great news, what's the first thing you do?

A Verse to Remember

This is love: not that we have loved God, but that he loved us and sent his Son to be the payment for our sins.

1 John 4:10

Longing to Be Well

Mark 5:25–34

I don't want to bother Jesus. But I'm sure if I could just touch the hem of his robe, I'd be healed, the sick woman thought.

Well, I've got nothing to lose. I've heard of the miracles Jesus has done and I believe he can heal me. The woman pushed her way through the crowd around Jesus. When she was near him, she dropped to her knees and touched the bottom of Jesus's robe. Instantly she felt something happen inside her.

Jesus stopped suddenly and asked, "Who touched me?"

"How can you ask that," his disciples said to him. There were hundreds of people around him. Fifty people had probably brushed against him in the last five minutes.

But Jesus said, "Someone just touched me in order to be healed. I felt power leave me."

The woman shrank back into the crowd. *Do I really think I can hide from him?* she thought. *He's God. I might as well speak up.* In a trembling voice, she said, "It was me. I've been sick for twelve years. I wanted to be well, and I knew that I would be if I just touched you."

Everyone was quiet as the woman explained what she had done. "When I touched your robe, I was healed," she said.

Jesus smiled gently before saying, "Your faith has made you well. Go live your life in peace."

When I touched your robe,

I was healed....

Becoming a Woman of God

A woman of God steps out in faith.

This woman had a lot of faith. She believed she could be healed just by touching the hem of Jesus's robe. He didn't need to touch her or pray for her or even speak to her.

Having faith means that you believe something is true even though you can't see it.

A Verse to Remember

Faith assures us of things we expect and convinces us of the existence of things we cannot see.

Hebrews 11:1

Giving My All

Mark 12:41–44

The old woman stood behind a pillar in the temple. *This is a time to praise God for all he has given me,* she thought. That was an interesting thought, coming from a woman whose husband was dead and who barely had any money.

The woman came to the temple every day to worship and praise God. Today she got in line to give her offering to God. The man ahead of her was dressed in a nice robe with fancy fringe around the edges.

He made a big show of putting his offering in the box. He made sure everyone was watching and he prayed loudly, but he didn't praise God at all. Instead, he told God how wonderful he himself was.

When it was her turn, the poor widow dropped two small coins into the offering box. The two coins together were barely worth a penny. After she put them in the box, the woman bowed her head and praised God for his many wonderful gifts to her. She prayed that her offering would be used to help those who were poorer and needier than she.

The woman didn't notice the rich men standing nearby who were laughing at her. But when she looked up, she saw Jesus standing across the room. Jesus knew that this poor woman had given everything she had for God's work. She could see the approval in his eyes.

Becoming a Woman of God

A woman of God is humble.

The poor woman was very generous. She gave all that she had for God's work.

She was also humble. That means that she didn't think she was more important than anyone else.

Do you enjoy being around people who talk about themselves all the time? How do you show others that you are humble?

A Verse to Remember

Don't act out of selfish ambition or be conceited. Instead, humbly think of others as being better than yourselves.

Philippians 2:3

The Gift of Life

Luke 7:11–17

When her son first got sick the worried mom prayed with all her heart, but her son died anyway. The pain in her heart was so great that she could feel nothing else. "It hurts so much. Where are you, God?" she prayed.

Somehow the boy's funeral was planned. The mom lived in a fog, hardly aware that friends were around her or that they were doing things for her. She was grateful for their help but couldn't even tell them how much it meant to her.

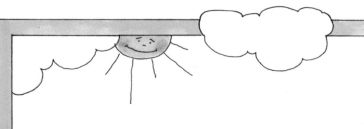

The day of the boy's funeral was warm and sunny, but the heartbroken mother didn't notice the sunshine or feel its warmth on her skin. Her friends walked with her as the funeral procession went through the town gate and toward the cemetery outside of town.

Outside the gate they met a group of men who had to wait for the procession to pass before they could go into town.

The mother walked slowly behind her son's coffin, her friends trying to comfort her. Suddenly a man's voice said, "Don't cry." The mourners looked at the man. They didn't understand how he could tell the heartbroken mother not to cry.

The gentle man went up to the boy's coffin and laid his hand on it. "Young man," he said, "get up!"

The mother stared at the man in disbelief. But when her son sat up, the grateful woman hugged her son—her only son. She looked into the face of Jesus, God's only Son, with tears running down her face. She praised God for his wonderful love and for giving her back her son.

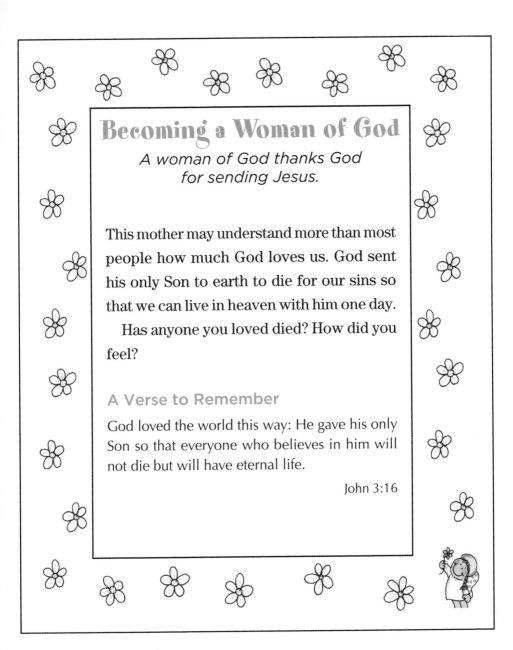

Becoming a Woman of God

*A woman of God thanks God
for sending Jesus.*

This mother may understand more than most people how much God loves us. God sent his only Son to earth to die for our sins so that we can live in heaven with him one day.

Has anyone you loved died? How did you feel?

A Verse to Remember

God loved the world this way: He gave his only Son so that everyone who believes in him will not die but will have eternal life.

John 3:16

Daddy's Girl

Mark 5:22-24, 35-43

"Don't worry, sweetheart. Everything will be okay,"
Jairus told his daughter. The little girl believed her daddy
could fix anything. For all her twelve years, he had taken
care of every problem she ever had. Then one day she
got very sick.

Her daddy had heard of a man named Jesus who did wonderful miracles—he healed sick people, and he even brought dead people back to life. Her daddy said he would go to get Jesus. She should just rest and wait for him to come back.

She was sure her daddy would be back soon with Jesus. She waited and waited, all the while getting sicker and sicker. Her momma stayed beside her and prayed for God to make her well. Before her daddy could return, the little girl died.

The little girl's mommy and grandparents cried. They sent a servant to tell the girl's father, Jairus, that it was too late because his little girl had died. When Jairus heard the news, he sadly turned and started home. But Jesus came with him, even though the girl was dead.

Later, Jairus held his little girl and told her how people had laughed when Jesus said she wasn't dead, she was just sleeping. But then Jesus had taken her hand and said, "Get up, little girl," and she did!

The little girl loved hearing the story. Jairus always ended the story by hugging her and thanking God for giving his daughter back to him.

Becoming a Woman of God

*A woman of God thanks God
for second chances.*

Jairus's daughter was given a second chance at life. No wonder she wanted to hear the story over and over! It showed her Jesus's amazing power and his love for her.

When have you been given a second chance at something? A wise person makes the most of second chances.

A Verse to Remember

God is faithful and reliable. If we confess our sins, he forgives them and cleanses us from everything we've done wrong.

1 John 1:9

A Gracious Hostess

Luke 10:38–42

Martha thought everything had to be perfect when she and Mary had company. There couldn't be a speck of dust in the whole house, the table had to be set, and dinner had to be ready exactly on time.

There couldn't be two more opposite people than Martha and her sister. Martha was a "doer" while Mary was a "thinker." When they had guests for dinner, Mary got so involved in talking to them that she'd forget to help Martha serve the meal.

When the sisters heard that Jesus was coming to visit them, Martha was very busy! She cleaned and cooked and worked right up to the minute Jesus came. Martha was making a wonderful dinner. She thought Mary would surely help her. But as soon as Jesus came in, Mary sat down to listen to his stories. Martha stomped off to the kitchen.

Martha mixed, stirred, and chopped. Every few minutes she peeked around the door to see if Mary was coming to help. She wasn't. In fact, each time Martha looked, Mary seemed to be deeper in conversation with Jesus. Pretty soon, Martha was really angry.

Finally, she could take it no longer. Marching in to Jesus, she said, "Tell Mary to get up and help me. I'd like to hear your stories too, but someone has to cook dinner."

Jesus was surprised at Martha's anger. He said, "Martha, you're so upset about your work. But Mary knows that talking to me is more important than anything. Forget the kitchen; let's talk."

Becoming a Woman of God

A woman of God knows what's most important.

It was important to Martha to have the house clean for Jesus's visit and to serve him a good meal. She meant well but Martha kept so busy that she missed the most important thing—spending time with Jesus.

Nothing should be more important than that.

A Verse to Remember

Carefully follow the commands and teachings that the LORD's servant Moses gave you. Love the LORD your God, follow his directions, and keep his commands. Be loyal to him, and serve him with all your heart and soul.

Joshua 22:5

Lazarus, Come Out!

John 11:1–45

Martha was preparing their brother for burial. She didn't act sad, but Mary knew she was. Working hard was Martha's way of handling her grief.

"Aren't you tired, Martha?" Mary asked.

"Yes, I am tired and disappointed that Jesus didn't come," Martha said with a sigh. "He could have helped Lazarus."

Mary was disappointed too.

The sisters had sent for Jesus when Lazarus got sick. They were sure he would come and heal their brother. But he didn't, and Lazarus died.

After Lazarus was buried, Mary and Martha went home. Relatives and friends came to comfort them. A few days later someone said, "Jesus is coming."

Martha ran to meet him. "My brother is dead," she told him. "If you had come when we sent for you, he would still be alive."

"Martha, those who believe in me are given eternal life. They will never die. Do you believe that?" Jesus asked.

"Yes," Martha said, "I know you are the Son of God."

"Where is Lazarus buried?" Jesus asked. Mary and Martha showed him the tomb.

"Move the stone," Jesus ordered. Martha was shocked. "But he has been dead four days already!" she said.

"Watch what God will do," Jesus answered. He looked up and prayed. Then he called, "Lazarus, come out!" Mary closed her eyes, but Martha didn't. When Martha gasped and squeezed her hand, Mary opened one eye. A man was standing in the cave's door, wrapped in grave clothes. Lazarus was alive!

Becoming a Woman of God

*A woman of God believes
in the resurrection of believers.*

Jesus taught an important lesson to Mary and Martha. People who believe in him know they will live forever. They may die on this earth, but they will be alive in heaven forever (with him!).

This is the promise of heaven. What do you think heaven will be like?

A Verse to Remember

I am the one who brings people back to life, and I am life itself. Those who believe in me will live even if they die.

John 11:25

Miracle of Mud

John 9:1–41

When the woman's son was born blind, she prayed,
"Please let my son see." But he remained blind. He had
to beg to earn his living when he became an adult.

One afternoon a crowd of Pharisees showed up, dragging the woman's son with them. Someone shouted, "Wasn't your son born blind? She started to answer, but another man shouted, "How can he see now?" She didn't know what to say. She wanted to ask her son what happened, but the Pharisees kept shouting, "Why can he see now?"

Peek-a-boo

Her husband came out and together they faced the crowd. "Yes, this is our son. Yes, he was born blind. We don't know why he can see now. He's an adult; ask him."

They listened as their son explained, "Jesus spit on the ground and made mud. Then he smeared the mud on my eyes. He told me to wash off the mud in the pool of Siloam. As soon as I did, I could see!"

Son, the worried mother thought, *be careful; these men don't like Jesus. They'll be angry that you're giving him credit for this.*

"How did he heal you?" the Pharisees kept asking.

Her son sighed. "I told you everything he did!"

She was afraid they would throw him in jail. But just then Jesus walked up. He turned to her son and asked, "Do you believe in the Son of Man?" The woman's heart sang as she saw her son fall to his knees and worship Jesus. "I believe," he said.

Becoming a Woman of God

*A woman of God is happy
when others come to know Jesus.*

If this mother knew Jesus, she would have been thrilled when her son believed in Jesus too. The Bible tells us that even the angels in heaven rejoice when just one person comes to know Jesus.

Every person is important to God. Can you picture the angels of heaven celebrating every time a person accepts Jesus as Savior? Have they celebrated for you yet?

A Verse to Remember

We love because God loved us first.

1 John 4:19

A Gift of Love

Luke 7:36-50

The woman watched men go into Simon's house. After a while she crept closer and peeked in an open window. The wonderful smell of food drifted out, finer food than she had ever eaten.

Her eyes roamed through the room until she found the one face she was looking for—Jesus. She had met him once before, and he had forgiven her sins.

The woman was so overwhelmed with love for Jesus that she did something amazing. Hurrying to her shabby home she took a beautiful jar from her cupboard. It was filled with expensive perfume, more special than anything else she owned and worth more money than all her other possessions put together.

She wrapped the jar in a cloth and hurried back to Simon's house. Before barging in, she took a deep breath. She went to Jesus and knelt at his feet.

The room became very quiet as the men watched tears run down the woman's face and fall on Jesus's feet. She gently wiped the tears away with her hair.

A loud gasp rolled through the room when she opened
the jar and poured the perfume on Jesus's feet.

Simon criticized Jesus for letting such a woman touch
him, but Jesus defended her. Her heart filled with love
for him. She had so much to be thankful for because
Jesus had forgiven her for so much.

Becoming a Woman of God

*A woman of God
is filled with love for Jesus.*

Jesus had forgiven this woman's sins when he had met her earlier. Because of Jesus's forgiveness, she was filled with love for him and she wanted to show him how very much she loved him.

How do you show people that you love them? How do you show God you love him?

A Verse to Remember

Jesus answered him, "Love the Lord your God with all your heart, with all your soul, and with all your mind."

Matthew 22:37

A Mother's
Broken Heart

John 19:1–30

Sometimes late at night Mary would look at the twinkling stars and remember when the shepherds and wise men had come to worship her child. She remembered old Simeon and Anna in the temple saying her baby was the Savior of the world, the promised Messiah.

Today, it became clear what they meant and her heart was breaking. Mary wanted to run through the streets of Jerusalem shouting, "Don't hurt him. He's my son!" Yet deep in her heart, she knew that the events of this day could not be stopped. Mary stood in the crowd as Jesus struggled to carry the heavy wooden cross.

She was swept along with the crowd to the hill called
Golgotha. She slid to the back of the crowd when the
soldiers threw Jesus to the ground and began pounding
the heavy spikes through his hands and feet and into the
wooden cross. With every clank of the hammer, Mary
wanted to turn and run, but she couldn't.

When the cross was dropped into the ground, Mary looked up at Jesus. She looked into his eyes, those gentle eyes that even on this horrible day were filled with love for the sinful people who had come to watch him die.

Mary knew the end was near when Jesus asked one of his friends to take care of her and she felt an arm slip around her shoulder.

When Jesus died, Mary fell to her knees, sobbing in pain.

Becoming a Woman of God

*A woman of God understands
Jesus's sacrifice.*

Mary was sad. It wasn't fair that the Son of God
was dying on a cross. Jesus left heaven to come
to earth and live. Even though he had done nothing wrong, he was killed as if he were a criminal.
He did all of this because of his great love for us.

How do you feel about what Jesus did for you?

A Verse to Remember

Believe in the Lord Jesus, and you and your family
will be saved.

Acts 16:31

A New Day Dawns

Luke 24:1–12

The three women got up early Sunday morning, before the sun rose. They were sad because Jesus had died.

They gathered spices and perfumes to put on Jesus's body. It was their custom to do this after a person had died. At first the women walked along in silence, each lost in her own sad thoughts.

How can we move it?

But as they neared the tomb, one woman spoke. "How are we going to move the stone?" she asked. The women stopped and looked at each other. They had been through so much in the last few days and they were exhausted. "How are we going to move the huge stone that covers the tomb door?" the woman asked, repeating her question.

The women were still worried about the stone when they reached the cave. Then the first woman shouted, "It's gone! The stone is gone—the tomb is open." They stared at the gaping doorway, more confused than ever.

Suddenly, an angel stood in front of them. "I know you're looking for Jesus," the angel said. "He isn't here. He came back to life, just as he said he would. Hurry to town and tell his friends."

For a second the women stood in silence, letting the angel's news sink in. Then they exploded with joy. "He's alive!" they shouted, running to find the disciples. "He's alive. Just as he said, he has come back to life!"

Becoming a Woman of God

A woman of God has hope.

These women thought all hope had died with Jesus. So the angel's announcement that Jesus was alive again brought hope back to their hearts.

Hope helps us through the hard times. If we believe that Jesus is alive, we share the same hope that the women in this story had.

Have you ever hoped for something? What was it?

A Verse to Remember

You are my hope, O Almighty LORD.
You have been my confidence ever since I was young.

Psalm 71:5

Mary of Magdala

John 20:10-18

The disciples went back to town, convinced that Jesus had risen from the dead. But Mary couldn't bring herself to leave the tomb. Had he really come back to life? If not, where was his body?

Mary wanted more than anything to believe that Jesus was alive. But there had been so many disappointments in the last few days, she was afraid to believe. After a while, she looked inside the tomb one last time.

The cave suddenly filled with light and Mary saw two beautiful angels. "Why are you crying?" they asked.

"Because someone has taken Jesus away, and I don't know where he is," she said. The angels left and Mary felt very alone.

Mary thought about things she wished she had told Jesus. He had forgiven her sins. She wished she had a chance to tell him how much that meant.

Then Mary saw a man standing nearby. "Sir, are you the gardener? Did you take Jesus's body away? Please tell me where you put him."

"Mary," he said.

Mary stared at the man until she realized it was Jesus!

Mary cried with joy, knowing that everything would be all right now.

Becoming a Woman of God

A woman of God grieves.

Mary was sad. Her hope was gone and she didn't try to hide it. God made us with feelings, so he understands when we are sad. If we try to pretend to God then we're not being honest with him.

When was a time you were very sad? Did you tell God about it?

A Verse to Remember

You will cry because you are sad, but the world will be happy. You will feel pain, but your pain will turn to happiness.

John 16:20

A Generous Seamstress

Acts 9:36-43

Nothing made Dorcas happier than helping someone who was poor. She wasn't a great cook or a wonderful teacher, but she was good at sewing. She loved to make nice clothes for people and was always sewing for someone.

When Dorcas started feeling sick, her friends tried to get her to slow down. "Take some time off; take a rest," they told her. But Dorcas kept stitching away. There was always one more person who could use a new robe or dress.

Dorcas's friends noticed that she was getting weaker and weaker. "Please, Dorcas, stop and rest," they pleaded.

But she wouldn't. "The Lord gave me a gift, and I'm going to use it," she said. One day, her friends found her dead, with her sewing needle still in her hands.

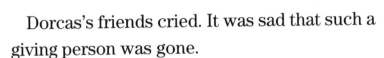

Dorcas's friends cried. It was sad that such a giving person was gone.

Then someone mentioned that Peter was nearby. "God has helped Peter do miracles. He has even raised people from the dead." Someone else said, "Let's send for him. Maybe he can do something!"

When Peter came, they showed him the clothing Dorcas had made for them. Peter sent them out of the room. Then he prayed and took Dorcas by the hand. "Get up," he ordered. Her eyes opened and she sat up, alive again! Peter called her friends to come back in. They all joyfully praised God for giving Dorcas back to them.

Becoming a Woman of God

A woman of God helps others.

Dorcas loved helping others by doing what she was best at—sewing. She cared about people and helped them in the best way she could.

Since Dorcas cared for others, she had many friends. Loving people are usually surrounded by friends.

Do you like to help other people? What do you enjoy doing to show others that you care about them?

A Verse to Remember

The message that you have heard from the beginning is to love each other.

1 John 3:11

New Life for Lydia

Acts 16:11–15

Lydia's business of selling purple dye was going well. She was thankful she didn't have to worry about money or food. When the Sabbath came, she could have used the time to rest. Instead, she usually joined a small group of women on the banks of the river outside town to worship.

One Sabbath morning, the women were gathered on the riverbank when they heard men's voices. Lydia looked up at the two men and recognized one as the apostle Paul. He traveled around the country teaching people about God. She wondered what he and his friend were doing there.

Paul prayed with the women and taught them about Jesus's death and resurrection. Lydia listened as Paul explained God's wonderful love. She had worshiped God but had never really understood him until now. Suddenly everything made sense.

Lydia asked Jesus to be her Savior. "Would you baptize me right now?" she asked Paul. They stepped into the river and Lydia said she believed in Jesus. Then Paul lowered her down into the water. After he lifted her out of the water, Lydia knew that she was a new person.

Lydia wanted to run into town and shout her new faith from the rooftops. She wanted to share all that she had. Turning to Paul, Lydia said, "You must come stay at my house. I have plenty of room. If you really believe that I'm a Christian now, please come." Paul happily accepted and went with her.

Becoming a Woman of God

A woman of God is God's friend.

The apostle Paul explained to Lydia the love and grace of God. As she listened to Paul, she probably wanted to know more and more about God.

The best way to become friends with someone is to spend time with that person and learn all you can about him or her.

How do you become a good friend of God's?

A Verse to Remember

Never stop praying.

1 Thessalonians 5:17

Sharing What You Know

Acts 18:18–28; Romans 16:3

Priscilla and her husband Aquila were tentmakers who spent time with the apostle Paul. He explained how Jesus died and came back to life and that after he went back to heaven he sent the Holy Spirit to help Christians.

Priscilla learned a lot from Paul, but sometimes she felt she wasn't doing her part in spreading the good news about God. She and Aquila promised each other to be braver about sharing their faith in God with others. They could tell their customers and even other tentmakers about him.

One time when Priscilla and Aquila were working in Ephesus, they heard a man named Apollos teaching about God. Priscilla listened to him for a while and then went to talk to her husband.

"Aquila," she said, "Apollos is teaching about John's baptism, but he doesn't know the rest of the story—the things that Paul taught us. He doesn't know about Jesus's death and resurrection. He doesn't know about the Holy Spirit. We have to tell him, Aquila. We know the whole story, and we should tell him."

"Why didn't you just go up and tell him?" Aquila asked.

"I didn't want to embarrass him in front of the people he was teaching," Priscilla said. "Let's invite him over for dinner, and we'll talk to him privately."

So Priscilla and Aquila invited Apollos over and told him the rest of the wonderful story. Now he could teach the whole truth about God's plan.

Becoming a Woman of God

*A woman of God is sensitive
to others' feelings.*

We don't really know why Priscilla didn't talk to Apollos in front of other people, but maybe she was being sensitive. Maybe she thought it would embarrass him in front of other people or that people would stop listening to his teaching.

How do you feel when someone embarrasses you on purpose?

A Verse to Remember

Always do for other people everything you want them to do for you. That is the meaning of Moses' Teachings and the Prophets.

Matthew 7:12

An Angel at the Door

Acts 12:12–17

Rhoda was a young servant girl. It was an honor for her to join the Christians' worship service. Tonight was a special prayer service for Peter, who was in prison. Peter's only crime was that he was a Christian.

Soft words of prayer filled the room as groups of people huddled together, praying for Peter's safety. Rhoda prayed as sincerely for Peter as everyone else did, but she was too shy to pray out loud. Late in the evening there was a knock on the door. Rhoda tried to concentrate on praying. But the knocking got louder and louder.

The noise was bothering other people, so Rhoda went to see who was at the door. When she opened it, she couldn't believe who was standing outside. She screamed and ran into the room. "It's Peter! Peter is at the door!" she shouted.

But no one believed her. "It can't be Peter. It must be his angel—he must already be dead!" people said. Then the knocking started again and everyone looked at Rhoda. So once again she went to the door. But this time she remembered to let Peter come in. Everyone stood and cheered when Peter walked in.

Peter gave Rhoda a little hug before he explained how God had sent an angel to lead him out of the prison. Rhoda listened to Peter's wonderful story of how God had miraculously freed him. She joined the others as they happily shouted, "Praise God!"

Becoming a Woman of God

A woman of God serves others.

Rhoda was a servant girl. Her job was to serve others.

Some think that successful people should have others do their jobs for them. But Jesus taught that his followers should serve others, not be served.

How can you serve others?

A Verse to Remember

It's the same way with the Son of Man. He didn't come so that others could serve him. He came to serve and to give his life as a ransom for many people.

Matthew 20:28

Bible Stories for
Mothers & Sons

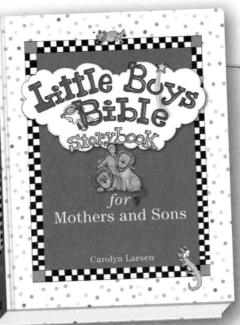

WITH WHIMSICAL AND COLORFUL ILLUSTRATIONS, and a large, easy-to-read font, these Bible storybooks will encourage quality quiet time with Mom and instill in boys a love for the Bible at a young age.